THE ROLE OF PROFESSIONAL DOCTORATES IN ADVANCING HIGHER EDUCATION AND WORK-BASED LEARNING

Applications in Health and Social Care

Carlo Lazzari   Elda Nikolou-Walker   Liang Liu

Grosvenor House
Publishing Limited

All rights reserved
Copyright © Carlo Lazzari, Elda Nikolou-Walker,
Liang Liu, 2024

The right of Carlo Lazzari, Elda Nikolou-Walker, Liang Liu
to be identified as the authors of this work has been
asserted in accordance with Section 78 of the
Copyright, Designs and Patents Act 1988

The book cover is copyright to Carlo Lazzari,
Elda Nikolou-Walker, Liang Liu

This book is published by
Grosvenor House Publishing Ltd
Link House
140 The Broadway, Tolworth, Surrey, KT6 7HT.
www.grosvenorhousepublishing.co.uk

This book is sold subject to the conditions that it shall not, by way of
trade or otherwise, be lent, resold, hired out or otherwise circulated
without the author's or publisher's prior consent in any form
of binding or cover other than that in which it is published and
without a similar condition including this condition being
imposed on the subsequent purchaser.

A CIP record for this book
is available from the British Library

Paperback ISBN 978-1-83615-003-9
Hardback ISBN 978-1-83615-004-6
eBook ISBN 978-1-83615-005-3

TABLE OF CONTENTS

TABLE OF CONTENTS iii
PREFACE v
INTRODUCTION vii
PROFESSIONAL DOCTORATES IN
HIGHER PSYCHIATRIC TRAINING 1
METHODS IN LITERATURE SEARCH 5
    Aim 5
    Book's questions 5
    Objectives 5
    Data extraction 6
CONTENT OF PROFESSIONAL
DOCTORATES 16
    Scopes of professional doctorates 16
    The methodology framework of DProf 19
    Middle-range theories 22
    Modes of knowledge production 23
    Critical incident analysis (CIA) 27
    Reflectivity 28

Reflexivity 31
Reflective practice and cycle 34
Autoethnography 35

GENERAL ASPECTS OF PROFESSIONAL DOCTORATES 38

IMPACT OF PROFESSIONAL DOCTORATES ON HIGHER EDUCATION IN HEALTH AND SOCIAL CARE 41

Enhancing Clinical Leadership Through Advanced Education 41
Impact on Healthcare Policy and Systems: A Closer Look 43
Challenges and Opportunities in Implementing Professional Doctorates 44
Future Directions for Professional Doctorates in Higher Education 46

PROFESSIONAL DOCTORATES BY PUBLIC WORKS 48

Understanding the Process of Earning a Professional Doctorate Through Publications 48

REFERENCES 52

PREFACE

Professional doctorates (DProf) are gaining popularity among advanced professionals, offering a unique opportunity to deepen their practical insights and drive organisational change. This narrative review of seminal articles and publications uncovers the theories and conceptual frameworks of DProf programmes and PhD/DProf degrees by publication. DProf pathways, with their qualitative interpretivist approach, integrate critical incident analysis, inductive methodology, autoethnography, self-reflective practice, and reflexivity, ensuring a successful thesis and programme completion. DProf degrees equip students to produce impactful scholarly research that informs policies and recommendations, directly addressing the challenges in their professional settings. Our focus is on the content of these programmes and their practical applicability in high psychiatric training and health and social care.

> The Authors,
> *Middlesex University*
> *London, June 2024*

INTRODUCTION

The rise in professional doctorate (DProf) courses worldwide is enhancing work-based learning, reflective practice skills, and implementing scholarly works. These programmes aid practitioners in bringing their data to policymaking, significantly impacting society. However, despite the popularity of these postgraduate courses, there are still limited studies exploring how to progress in these degrees and create the required dissertations successfully.

Professional growth is a crucial focus of the Master and Doctor of Professional Studies (MProf/DProf) degrees, emphasising study inquiry in a professional setting and fostering critical reflection and career advancement through practice-based research projects (Middlesex University, 2024). Beginning with a professional practice problem that requires investigation and answers is typical for professional doctorate research (Bourner et al., 2001). DProf candidates start with the unknown (professional practice problems) with far-reaching implications (Bourner et al., 2001). DProf learning outcomes include (1) the ability to make a significant unique contribution to professional practice knowledge through research, (2) personal growth through reflective practice or writing, (3) professional-level knowledge of a broad area of study, (4) professionalism in the student's field of practice, and (5) awareness of the importance of research to senior professional practitioners (Bourner et al., 2001).

DProf postgraduate programmes employ a reflective approach to address workplace complexities and help students change their practice settings (Costley, 2011). DProf students analyse their settings and progress to innovative contributions through a thesis. DProf programmes thus promote professional growth and advancement, resulting in products, publications, systems, or frameworks to bring about change in the candidate's organisation or practice (Costley, 2011). DProf research candidates must also make a significant contribution to their settings of practice and be innovative: (1) they use job-related learning objectives, (2) cohort-based pedagogies, (3) professional growth, and (4) they aim to develop plans to improve practice in their connected professions (Jones, 2018). Work-based learning (WBL) is the backbone that allows the successful completion of DProf programmes.

The tasks assigned to participants will include: (1) critically analysing a work-related scenario or theme to a negotiated brief using appropriate methods; (2) solving pertinent structured problems individually and, if appropriate, in groups; (3) reporting on learning gained from the project in an appropriate narrative style; (4) suggesting guidelines for change based on the project findings; (5) critically reflecting on experience and/or practice; (6) independently researching and evaluating their performance (Nikolou-Walker and Garnett, 2004).

PROFESSIONAL DOCTORATES IN HIGHER PSYCHIATRIC TRAINING

The landscape of higher education in psychiatry is witnessing a transformative shift, particularly with the increasing recognition and integration of professional doctorates (Lasuertmer, 2024). These advanced degrees, such as the Doctor of Psychology (PsyD) and the Doctorate in Clinical Psychology (DClinPsy), represent a pivotal evolution in preparing practitioners for the complex challenges of mental health care (Writers, 2024). Introducing professional doctorates in psychiatry marks a significant departure from traditional academic pathways, focusing more on practical skills, clinical expertise, and applied research (Park et al., 2023). This transition underscores a broader commitment to enhancing psychiatric practice through innovative educational frameworks.

Professional doctorates in psychiatry are designed with an explicit aim: to bridge the gap between theoretical knowledge and clinical application (MacLean, 2024). This is achieved by emphasising experiential learning, where students engage directly with patients under supervision, developing diagnostic and therapeutic competencies essential for effective practice (University of Dayton, 2024). Unlike their purely academic counterparts, which primarily concentrate on generating new knowledge through research, professional doctorates equip students with a robust skill set tailored for immediate application in clinical settings (Loma Linda University, 2024).

The curriculum of these programmes is meticulously crafted to reflect the multidimensional nature of psychiatric disorders (Amsalem, Duvivier and Martin, 2021). It combines foundational subjects such as psychopathology, pharmacology, and neuroscience with specialised training in psychotherapeutic techniques, ethics, and cultural competence (University of Miami, 2024). This comprehensive approach ensures that graduates are not only proficient in assessing and treating mental illnesses but are also sensitive to the diverse backgrounds and needs of their patients (University of Nevada, 2022).

Moreover, professional doctorates introduce candidates to applied research methodologies relevant to healthcare practice (MacLean, 2024). This aspect is crucial for fostering evidence-based interventions that can adapt to evolving healthcare landscapes (University of Ohio, 2024). Students learn how to evaluate existing literature critically, design studies addressing real-world clinical questions, and implement findings to improve patient outcomes (New Mexico State University, 2024a). Such skills are invaluable for advancing care and contributing to the field's body of knowledge (American Association of College of Nursing, 2024).

Including professional practice elements within these programmes also prepares graduates for leadership roles within healthcare services (University of Southern

California, 2024). They emerge as advocates for change, with insights into service design and delivery that promote accessibility and quality of care for all individuals affected by health issues (George Washington University, 2024).

In conclusion, professional doctorates signify an essential progression in healthcare education by aligning academic rigour with practical difficulties (Regis College, 2023). They serve not only as conduits for personal career advancement but also as engines driving the quality and efficacy of health services globally (Online Counseling Programs, 2024). As such programmes continue to evolve and expand their reach, they promise to play a critical role in shaping future generations of health carers adept at navigating clinical complexities and societal expectations within an ever-changing healthcare environment (Ross et al., 2015).

METHODS IN LITERATURE SEARCH

Aim

The book's rationale was to explore the theoretical and practical aspects of professional doctorate (DProf) degrees and the structure of the required dissertations.

Book's questions

(1) What are the characteristics of professional doctorates?
(2) How can DProf programmes disentangle and resolve complexities in candidates' settings through work-based learning and reflective learning?

Objectives

(1) To conduct a narrative review of major theories and practices related to professional doctorate programmes.

(2) To extract the methodologies and methods for completing professional doctorate dissertations from relevant literature.

Data extraction

A total of 70 peer-reviewed journal articles, including also books, book chapters and Internet sources in English, were comprised in the narrative review. The review was conducted at Middlesex University from September 2023 to March 2024. Search engines were PubMed, PsychINFO, Scopus, Web of Science, Google Scholar, Google, EMBASE, and others. Boolean connectives 'AND', 'OR' linked the keyword search. Search words were 'professional doctorate*', 'methodology', 'DProf', 'work-based learning', 'interpretivism', 'critical incident*', 'critical incident analysis', 'Kolb's reflective cycle', 'reflectivity', 'reflexivity', 'middle range theory', 'qualitative analysis', 'autoethnography', 'PhD OR DProf by public work', 'PhD OR DProf by publication', 'PhD OR by published work'. Two independent researchers (CL and EN-W) scrutinised relevant papers, while the third reviewer (LL) supervised the choice when there was a conflict of opinion between the first two reviewers. We selected articles in English that were comprehensive of a full test. The study started in September 2023 and ended in March 2024.

A PRISMA flowchart helped select and choose papers (Page et al., 2021; Table I). To conduct the narrative review, we used meta-synthesis, including (1) mutual translation: ideas from one research was included in another, and (2) synthesis of the line of argument: studies that have shown different aspects of the topic were combined to form a new perspective (Booth, 2006). One of the steps of the meta-synthesis is to compare the studies with each other and generate a final summary of the results (Noblit and Hare, 1988).

Incorporating these findings into policy, programme creation, and research is one approach to synthesising a literature search (Noblit and Hare, 1988). A literature review aims to blend in-depth relevant research and make generalisable statements based on the theories generated by such research (Noblit and Hare, 1988). Since this is a narrative review, we also applied the Arksey and O'Malley method for bibliographic analysis, which includes stages such as (1) clarifying and connecting the purpose and the research question, (2) using qualitative thematic analysis when reviewing articles, and (3) considering the implications of the study findings for policy, practice, or research (Levac et al., 2010). Other relevant sources were grey literature and Internet sources, which can provide a broader perspective on DProf by capturing the local and university philosophy in promoting such programmes.

Table I. Summary of findings in the extracted literature

Author	*Summary points and theories of professional doctorates.*
Middlesex University, 2024	A DProf permits experienced professionals who have made noteworthy contributions to organisations and professional growth to compose a targeted evaluation and context statement of their achievements.

Bourner et al., 2001	The outcome of DProf is to produce original work that advances practice.
Costley, 2011	DProf aims to advance scholarship to help candidates bring a change in their organisations and stakeholders.
Jones, 2018	DProf candidates make an innovative contribution to their professional areas of expertise.
Orlans, 2014	DProf programmes aim to advance professional knowledge, improve professional practice, and promote the advancement of methods for work-based reflection.
O'Keeffe, 2019	A DProf by portfolio includes previously published works, such as journal articles, books, book chapters, and other public works.
Butt, 2013	DProf programmes allow candidates who have already published in their field of interest to be recognised at higher academic levels.

Mullane, 2005	The target beneficiary (usually a patient, healthcare provider, or public or private service provider) is the goal of the change that DProf candidates aim to generate.
Rolfe and Davies, 2009	Professional doctorates promote Gibbon's Mode 2 knowledge production by using research to solve problems in the candidate's community of practice.
Powell and Green, 2007	Candidates use and condense their published research (if any) by using a narrative or summary demonstrating a candidate's independent thinking.
Green et al., 2005	The academic work for DProf is a synthesis, commentary, summary, assessment, or critical essay.
Badley, 2009; Peacock, 2017	The document that unifies the published works in DProf by PW (professional doctorate by public works) is the text that accompanies the publications.

Fulton et al., 2019	A DProf and its context statement project are extracted from the candidate's settings to demonstrate its impact on the employer and community of practice.
Enders, 2005	While compiling a DProf dissertation, candidates should clarify their research positionality.
Weingart, 1998	Disseminating research findings through media can increase the reach and impact of research findings in DProf.
Fulton et al., 2019	Candidates write in the first person 'I' in their DProf context statement as a reflective practice.
Smith, 2015	A dissertation in a DProf by PW (Professional Doctorate by Public Works) is a qualitative analysis of the candidate's former publications.
Fulton et al., 2019	Candidates use an interpretivist qualitative approach to analyse their portfolio, compiling the requirements of a DProf by PW to promote change.

Lazzari, Costley and Nikolou-Walker, 2024	By using a qualitative interpretivist approach, the candidate aims to the transferability of findings in similar clinical contexts.
Leeman and Sandelowski, 2012; Bradley et al., 2004	DProf context statements can aim to craft middle-range theories and, by using qualitative research methods, can help implement interventions in the real world as target policies.
Coast and Jackson, 2017; Blaikie and Priest, 2017	DProf candidates, in their context statement, use a process of abduction to answer 'how' and 'why' questions of their professional practice.
Lazzari, Costley and Nikolou-Walker, 2024	DProf candidates can use autoethnography, storytelling, and critical incident analysis extracted from their clinical practice setting.
de Oliveira et al., 2015; Cartwright, 2020	Middle-range theories (as often aimed at in DProf context statements) can help theorise findings that candidates extract from their clinical practice settings.

Gibbons et al., 1994	It is often reported that DProf context statements aim for Mode 2 knowledge production outside academia in the researcher's community of practice.
Del Giudice et al., 2011	A new form of knowledge production in the DProf context statement is Mode 3 knowledge production, which involves knowledge that develops at individual, organisational, and systemic levels.
Fulton et al., 2019	DProf candidates use critical incident analysis to reflectively explore how a critical incident has influenced the candidate's professional practice and course of action.
Fulton et al., 2019	DProf context statements are based on a constructionist methodology of analysis of candidates' events extracted from practice.
Gibbons et al., 1994	Desired knowledge production is achieved in the utilisation settings through an interdisciplinary approach to resolve problems actively.

Carayannis and Campbell, 2012	DProf leverages feedback from major stakeholders to promote implementation in the researcher's community of practice. Changes and knowledge can progress from individual to organisational to global scenarios.
Francis, 1997; Richards and Farrell, 2005	Critical incident analysis helps to disentangle a problem and explore alternative solutions through self-reflective practice.
Malthouse et al., 2014; Mortari, 2015; Dahlberg et al., 2013; Ben-Ari and Enosh, 2010	The ability to view and think about one's activities from 'outside' aligns with becoming aware of how DProf candidates can reflect on their personal experiences to construct the meaning of their practice. The student-researcher turns back to the self, where he or she is both the observed and the observer. While the experience occurs, the student-researcher identifies critical incidents in their community of practice and the ethical and practical paths to deal with them.

Dodgson, 2019; Berger, 2013; Salzman, 2002	Reflexivity is recognising and exploring how personal beliefs and positionality can impact research. Reflexivity is a conscious effort to be cognisant of one's reactions to the subject/object of investigation.
Kolb, 2015	A self-reflective cycle comprehends concrete experience, reflective observation, abstract conceptualisation, and active experimentation.
Poulos, 2021; Adams et al., 2022	Autoethnography is the use of self-reflective writing where the researcher uses memory work or published articles to analyse personal cultural beliefs and values through thick descriptions of settings, stakeholders, and events and self-reflective and reflexive practice. The student researchers aim to make sense of their daily practice via a narrative.

CONTENT OF PROFESSIONAL DOCTORATES

Scopes of professional doctorates

A professional doctorate (DProf) is a programme that allows professionals to qualify alongside their work and base a project on their workplace; the project is extracted from the candidate's practice, based on activities, helps develop their practice, and requires evidence of the impact of their work on employers and the broader community (Fulton et al., 2019).

According to Orlans (2014), professional knowledge (and work-based learning) encompasses a systematic accumulation of philosophical and theoretical perspectives aiming at a critical grasp of knowledge and the capacity to produce new relevant information. Researchers conduct new, practitioner-led research to address cutting-edge issues, critique current methodologies, demonstrate ethical thinking, and generate publishable ideas and conclusions (Orlans, 2014). Orlans (2014) adds that practitioner attributes include taking charge of professional concerns, handling complicated circumstances ethically, contributing to their field, and developing confidence and personal growth.

Professional Doctorates by Public Works (DProf by PW) are rapidly expanding in the UK. DProf by PW applicants must show that their contextualisation statement and public works (journals, books, book chapters, and other portfolios) meet degree requirements (O'Keeffe, 2019) as they will generate a commentary on these as a thesis route.

The DProf by PW aims to recognise professionals like health and business professionals, creative writers, and researchers who have published or are currently conducting research at the highest academic level (Butt, 2013). The focus should be on enhancing an individual's professional capability, meeting current and future professional or multi-professional group needs, and addressing the primary recipients (stakeholders) of research outcomes (Mullane, 2005). DProf by PW offers practitioners the opportunity to work in a university context, transforming their professionally acknowledged practice into academic currency and promoting Mode 2 knowledge production by solving problems in their settings of practice (Rolfe and Davies, 2009).

Green et al. (2005) highlight the diverse naming conventions for narratives (abridging candidates' published work), such as criticism, critical essay, synthesis, commentary, summary, or assessment referring to the thesis in these programmes; the narrative should highlight the publications' contributions to the field's knowledge and demonstrate a candidate's independent, creative capacity.

The document that unifies submitted articles or papers and provides a compelling critical narrative is also called an 'explanation', supplying an exploratory text (or exploratory qualitative method) that explains them (Green et al., 2005; Badley, 2009; Peacock, 2017).

The methodology framework of DProf

According to the reflective practice tradition, a professional doctoral thesis uses the first person 'I' in the storyline (Fulton et al., 2019). A DProf by PW is usually structured as a *qualitative (exploratory) analysis of former public works and publications* (Smith, 2015). Professional doctorates involve researchers immersing themselves in work-based learning to promote changes arising from discovering inequalities or conundrums in their practice settings (Fulton et al., 2019).

Often applying a qualitative research approach, DProf learning usually focuses on a small sample of people (or on a portfolio of public works) in the settings of students' practice, aiming for the *transferability* of research findings in similar scenarios using detailed descriptions of professional situations (Fulton et al. 2019; Lazzari, Costley and Nikolou-Walker, 2024). Hence, in the process that leads to the development of a professional doctorate and the relative context statement (CS) or thesis, candidates use an *interpretivist methodology*: (1) the *axiology* intended by a

CS or its ethical and social goal is to raise awareness and develop democratic participation of stakeholders; (2) the *ontology* is the nature of reality which is relativism, that is, acknowledging multiple and subjective interpretations of social realities of persons who dynamically present into learners' settings of practice; (3) the *settings* and definitions are thus contextual; both service users and service providers dynamically generate meanings and expectations according to underlying needs, with demands and interventions moulded by their personal worldviews; (4) the *epistemology* and methods for a DProf research that compiles a CS is usually interactive with the researcher as a participant-observer of the settings (work-based practice) *using tacit knowledge and thick descriptions to extrapolate applicative middle-range theories of the own whereabouts*; (5) the *methodology* of a CS on its own is *interpretive* with logical and well-described contexts which allow the transferability of the findings to similar settings (Lazzari, Costley and Nikolou-Walker, 2024; Collis and Hussey, 2014).

Therefore, a CS and a DProf might reflect and align with the qualitative research methods examining the 'how' and 'why' of decision making rather than the 'when', 'what', and 'where'; qualitative inquiry also aims to explore, narrate, and explain social phenomena and make sense of the complex human reality (Renjith et al., 2021). CS-produced qualitative research seeks to generate practice-based actions and real-world implementation techniques (Leeman and Sandelowski, 2012).

DProf curriculum enables candidates to develop novel insights, ideas, and applications from their everyday practice and inductively apply them to comparable situations or invite others to do likewise (Leeman and Sandelowski, 2012). Qualitative research (often used to compile a CS) helps explain causal processes, construct a theory, and implement policies in the learners' settings (Bradley et al., 2004).

DProf researchers should also ponder local/regional trends to build new hypotheses and test them inductively (Coast and Jackson, 2017). Thus, DProf trainees use *induction* to create theories to answer 'why' and 'how' questions by explaining associations between phenomena observed in their professional practice and extracting possible regularities and relationships (Blaikie and Priest, 2017).

Middle-range theories

Another goal in DProf dissertations is to craft middle-range theories (MRTs) that are extractable from the researcher's community of practice. MRTs are divided into (1) descriptive MRTs, which categorise phenomena based on a single concept, (2) explanatory MRTs, which examine the connections between ideas and their nature, and (3) predictive MRTs, which aim to explain and predict changes within a phenomenon by identifying specific links between ideas or deeds, or the impacts of one or more concepts in patterns (Fawcett and Garity, 2009; De Oliveira et al., 2015; Cartwright, 2020). MRTs link theoretical concepts of frameworks.

A theoretical concept is a verbal expression of reality that defines and clarifies the meaning of an occurrence relevant to a writer's field, often referred to as a theoretical framework which organises related ideas to characterise and clarify phenomena (Smith et al., 2024).

The development of middle-range theories originates from clinical experience and clinical practice standards (Peterson and Bredow, 2020). Therefore, MRT is a basic, usable structure of ideas (Smith et al., 2024).

A theoretical concept is an idea of a reality that is expressed verbally to define and clarify the meaning of an occurrence relevant to the writer's field (Smith et al., 2024). Cognate to MRTs is a theoretical framework that is an arrangement of related ideas that characterise and clarify the impact of phenomena (Smith et al., 2024).

A theory is (1) a broad concept that makes sense and supports science, (2) used to explain phenomena, (3) a collection of connected concepts that aim to explain or forecast related occurrences, and (4) these rationally connected concepts make sense in light of empirical data, leading to more empirical correlations (Merriam-Webster Dictionary, 2024a; American Psychological Association, 2024a).

Modes of knowledge production

The theory of reflective context in DProf involves autoethnography and reflectivity, aiming to describe clinical realities and complexities; this approach aligns with a constructionist strategy, focusing on small-scale studies for theory generation and reflection, thereby supporting professional doctorates and MRTs construction (Fulton et al., 2019).

The aim of DProf candidates is knowledge production, usually according to two primary modes. *Gibbons Mode-2-of-knowledge-production* is shaped in the researcher's context and justified by practical, cooperative, and transdisciplinary routes where the investigator is a socially responsible, engaged, and reflexive player or change proxy (Gibbons et al., 1994).

Mode 2 knowledge production (1) is produced in the *setting of utilisation* following the guidelines of the practice that governs a particular discipline and problem solving, focused around a specific purpose; (2) is *transdisciplinary* as although the knowledge was generated in a particular setting, it develops its own unique theoretical construction, research methods and way of application, thus, through a cumulative effect it can be applied into different directions; (3) is *heterogeneous* in that it has a high number of potential settings where knowledge can be generated; (4) is *socially accountable and reflexive* as researchers are active agents in the description and resolution of problems, but through reflexivity, they evaluate their functioning and the impact of their research is analysed from its beginning, and (5) *quality controlled* means that the outcome is of social interest and determines if the research will be socially suitable (Gibbons et al., 1994).

For example, our study of a mental health condition, a personality disorder, in Mode 2 knowledge, aimed to understand health promotion behaviours, inequities, resource shortages, and patient conflict management in various healthcare settings. It was applied in infectious disease departments, psychiatric units, general hospitals, liaison psychiatric teams, and community mental health teams. The reflective method explored philosophical, professional, and moral ideas influencing the observed and understood phenomena.

Carayannis and Campbell Mode 3 knowledge production emphasises that knowledge modes coexist and evolve consensually at the individual (micro or local), structural and organisations (meso or institutional), and systemic (macro or global) levels (Del Giudice et al., 2011). By adopting a *Mode 3 knowledge production*, a researcher aims to generate outcomes on a 'quadruplex helix' by joining the own academic progress, analysing the own settings of practice, involving external organisations interested in the topics and applications of his findings, and aiming from feedback from major stakeholders (such as health carers, public health planners, social services) to promote identified plans for desired implementation in the own settings of practice (Carayannis and Campbell, 2012).

Using Mode 3 knowledge, we saw a personality disorder (borderline personality disorder) as (1) a pathology in early childhood attachment that affects health behaviours in adulthood (micro) (Lazzari and Masino, 2015), (2) causing organisational conflicts with primary carers, the health system, and health resources (meso) (Lazzari and Shoka, 2016a, b), and (3) having a systemic effect on population health such as hospital bed reduction or limited national healthcare resources for other pathologies as saturated by this personality disorder (macro) (Lazzari et al., 2021).

Critical incident analysis (CIA)

DProf candidates must demonstrate (1) what critical incident they consider significant in their profession and how it affects their values and behaviours, (2) critically analyse this incident using the literature and conjectures before, during, and after the incident, and (3) reflect on how the critical analysis has shaped their knowledge and behaviour (Fulton et al., 2019). A CIA addresses fundamental concerns such as (1) what is happening, (2) how others may interpret it differently, (3) what alternative behaviours are possible, and (4) who benefits or suffers (Francis, 1997).

A narrative reflection enhances CIA (Farrell, 2013). Critical moments occur when the narrator deliberately evaluates their work and obtains fresh ideas for solving critical incidents (CIs) (Richards and Farrell, 2005). CIs are sudden, overwhelming events and often detrimental to oneself or a loved one (Schwester et al., 2012). CIs are unique experiences that shock our systems, test our coping mechanisms, and drive us to adjust to the harsh reality that has affected our lives (Schwester et al., 2012). CIs are significant events that transcend a person or group's usual coping strategies (Schwester et al., 2012). CIs are abrupt, decisive, and unusual, so even well-trained individuals are emotionally affected (Kirby, 2012).

CIs in healthcare are acute, unexpected, or chronic events that recently worsened into a sub-acute condition and impact both service users and providers, who endeavour to identify a shared care pathway to restore patient and carer satisfaction and safety (Lazzari and Shoka, 2016a, b). CIs and organisational changes impact healthcare professionals, patients, the organisation, and the community equally (Lazzari, Costley and Nikolou-Walker, 2024).

Reflectivity

Reflectivity is a process linked to one's work-based learning and is the skill to reflect on practice that practitioners use to improve and advance their work (Malthouse et al., 2014).

To acquire a capacity to establish a generalised theory about their actions in comparable circumstances, practitioners are encouraged to reflect on CIs that have occurred in their practice; this happens through the ability to view and think about one's activities from 'outside', which is one aspect of the external perspective (Malthouse et al., 2014).

Thus, since the researchers' thinking shapes the whole inquiry process, they must clarify their reasoning to make the heuristic process responsible and legitimate (Mortari, 2015). Furthermore, since researcher-observers form part of the observed phenomena, they are accountable for each act of ethnographic inquiry (Mortari, 2015). Thus, if the researchers' mental experience conditions the study by introducing the subjective gaze into the heuristic process, they should take a self-reflective posture by declaring their position (Dahlberg et al., 2013).

The aim is to become aware of how their framework implicitly conditions the research process (Dahlberg et al., 2013). In research, reflective practice helps subjects improve self-awareness by focusing on how the self impacts the research project (Dahlberg et al., 2013). Hence, reflective researchers/ practitioners know what organises their mental lives and how these cognitive artefacts shape their enquiry (Mortari, 2015). John Dewey coined the term 'reflection' to describe active, persistent, and careful self-awareness of any researcher's belief or supposed form of knowledge by considering its grounds and the further conclusions it tends to, including a conscious and voluntary effort to establish an idea (or theory) on a firm basis of evidence and rationality (cited in Ben-Ari and Enosh, 2010).

Reflection is thus the active and aware process that emphasises the researcher's dual position inside and outside the phenomena, necessitating ongoing movement between the two (Ben-Ari and Enosh, 2010). *Reflectivity entails considering how our values, experiences, interests, beliefs, and political views form our identities* (Ben-Ari and Enosh, 2010) *and how these affect our research methods and resulting outcomes* (Collis and Hussey, 2014).

Reflectivity also requires awareness of one's social background and how cultural and ideological mind frames affect previously assumed actions (Lazzari et al., 2024). Ethnographic researchers are typically participants and spectators of the phenomena they study; thus, researchers must assess their positionality relative to the phenomena investigated and others (Ben-Ari and Enosh, 2010).

Reflexivity

Reflexivity pertains to the comprehension of the intricate connections between people and social systems on both a micro and macro scale; that is, it represents the ability of a person to place him/herself within the more significant social and organisational causes of specific issues (Malthouse et al., 2014).

Researchers must pay close attention to their self-awareness and sensitivity, comprehend the role of the self in knowledge generation, keep a close eye on how their prejudices, beliefs, and life experiences affect their work, and strike a balance between the particular and the universal (Berger, 2013). When examining the similarities and differences between the researcher and the study participants, it is crucial to know whether the researchers are insiders or outsiders and whether they have shared their experiences with the subjects in their research (Berger, 2013).

As a result, the researcher has to be aware of these parallels and differences and inform the readers about them (Dodgson, 2019). The capacity of the researcher(s) to explain these parallels and contrasts to readers and participants, as well as to themselves, will determine the quality of the study (Dodgson, 2019).

Researchers must be cognisant of unconscious biases (e.g., racism and sexism) that might affect the lens of their investigation (Dodgson, 2019). When a researcher uses an established theoretical framework to evaluate qualitative data, there is always a danger that this framework will restrict (or expand) what the researcher can 'see' in the data (Dodgson, 2019).

To acknowledge and accept responsibility for one's *situatedness* within the research and its potential effects on the environment and subjects being researched, the questions being asked, the data being collected, and its interpretation is reflexivity, meaning turning the researcher's lens back onto oneself (Berger, 2013).

Reflexivity thus helps identify and explain potential or actual effects of personal, contextual, and circumstantial aspects on the research process and study findings; it also maintains the researchers' awareness of themselves as part of the world they study (Dodgson, 2019). *Reflexivity is thus a researcher's conscious and deliberate effort to be attuned to one's reactions to respondents, the object/subject of investigation, and how the research account is constructed* (Berger, 2013).

Reflexivity in ethnographic research is an approach to recognising and discovering a researcher's self-knowledge, opinions, skills, and impact on research (Salzman, 2002). As researchers and academics, we authors know that our educational background, career positionality, generational beliefs, and areas of expertise might impact the cogent themes we extract from our research, including recommendations and concerns. All these factors are influenced by our job position, years of experience in the topic treated, number of publications that have endorsed our outcomes, and level of influence on our organisations.

Reflective practice and cycle

The work-based practice uses several self-reflective cycles. Bassot (2016) defines Knor and Scrabb's reflective writing model as (1) reflecting on our profession and growth, (2) analysing the issue, alternative ways to consider it, and how this affects our beliefs, and (3) acting on what we learned and what we would do next. Schön suggested that professional knowledge is the viewpoint from which practitioners mould their professional response (cited in Thompson and Thompson, 2018).

Kolb's (2015) reflective cycle can be chosen to craft a self-reflective CS: (1) *Concrete Experience* represents the experiencing of the event, which is the researcher's concern; (2) *Reflective Observation* is about reflecting on the experience; (3) *Abstract Conceptualisation* entails thinking and theorising about the event of concern, and (4) *Active Experimentation* is about acting as a consequence of the above processes, e.g. through proposed changes and policies. The goal of experiential learning theory is to allow individuals to take control of their experiences and master them while reinforcing the individuality of each practitioner, encouraging them to express their uniqueness for the benefit of society (Kolb, 2015).

Autoethnography

DProf candidates can use autoethnography to craft their CS (Lazzari et al., 2024). Autoethnography consists of (1) the 'auto', where the researcher uses his or her artefacts, published work, and formative and challenging life experiences through time, space, and circumstances to challenge institutional ways of doing things and offer lessons to improve life, (2) the 'ethnic', where the researcher self-reflectively analyses his or her cultural beliefs, values, practices, and identities to ask and answer questions, and (3) the 'graphy' where the researcher applies his or her experiences to generate reachable, tangible, and suggestive thick descriptions of cultural life, settings of practice, and viable solutions (Adams et al., 2022).

Daily reflective writing helps autoethnographers comprehend their reality and construct a research-based story using observations, arguments, artefacts, and recollections to explain daily life while engaging in emotional, intellectual, spiritual, holistic, performative, social, and dialogical writing (Poulos, 2021). Autoethnographers observe, participate, journal, and collect field notes to study human social life's obstacles and appeal as extracted from their settings while trying to combine, analyse, interpret, and tell captivating stories (Poulos, 2021).

An autoethnography includes personal, interpersonal, and transpersonal tales, researcher's interactions with service users, and how these reflected on the researcher and his or her community of practice (Lazzari, Costley and Nikolou-Walker, 2024). Autoethnography can become compelling tales to properly represent a historical reality that meets modern factual evidence about an event, crisis, or experience (Denzin, 2014). Autobiographical statements are also a mix of fiction and nonfiction because each narrative account includes specific, individual truths or verisimilitudes about life and personally lived experiences; autoethnography represents a creative organisation of experience that imposes truth (Denzin, 2014).

GENERAL ASPECTS OF PROFESSIONAL DOCTORATES

DProf candidates use work-based learning to improve their community of practice by introducing new ideas and policies. The sociologist Robert Merton defines middle-range theories as theories that fall between the many minor but essential working hypotheses that arise in daily research and the methodical attempts to create a single theory that accounts for all observed uniformities in social behaviours, organisations, and social changes (Encyclopedia.Com, 2024).

Divergent thinking (or abduction) in DProf courses may boost creativity and problem solving since ideas are distinctive (Runco and Pritzker, 2011). Abductive conclusions develop new hypotheses from known components, facts, or knowledge (Merriam-Webster Dictionary, 2024a). Work-based learning and inductive inquiry favour abductive thinking. Diversity (or inventiveness) creates discoveries or new challenges (Encyclopaedia Britannica, 2024). Creative problems need adaptation, ingenuity, fluency, and insight (Encyclopaedia Britannica, 2024). Innovations disrupt old ways of thinking and doing and add new value to existing problems (Samuel and Stokes, 2023).

Combinatory innovation reinvents existing concepts (Samuel and Stokes, 2023). Therefore, mental uniqueness generates innovation, not history (Samuel and Stokes, 2023). Creative ideas are sudden ('Eureka' phenomenon) (Samuel and Stokes, 2023). Therefore, innovative practice results from DProf dissertations that can generate a gestalt change in the researcher's community. Scientific discoveries begin with a phenomenon that defies nature and paradigms (Kuhn, 1962).

Further inquiry into an abnormal situation leads to paradigm changes, and the unexpected becomes the norm (Kuhn, 1962). Therefore, imaginative researchers need empirical and theoretical uniqueness to advance science (Kuhn, 1962).

Kuhn (1962) describes a scientific revolution as a gestalt shift transforming scientific practice and forcing scientists to retrain their discernments and sense a new gestalt in familiar contexts.

Gestalt is the overall character of anything and a physical, biological, or psychological phenomenon ordered or structured to produce a working unit with attributes that cannot be achieved by adding the components (Merriam-Webster Dictionary, 2024b).

Gestalt is a united structure or experience (Cambridge Dictionary, 2024). Scientific discoveries are gestalt because they begin with an anomaly that challenges nature and paradigms (Kuhn, 1962). Scientists examine anomalous situations until the paradigm changes and the unexpected becomes routine, advancing science experimentally and conceptually (Kuhn, 1962).

Gestalt is the overall quality or character of everything and a physical, biological, or psychological phenomenon ordered or structured to produce a working unit with features that cannot be obtained by combining the individual components (Merriam-Webster Dictionary, 2024c; Cambridge Dictionary, 2024; American Psychological Association, 2024b).

IMPACT OF PROFESSIONAL DOCTORATES ON HIGHER EDUCATION IN HEALTH AND SOCIAL CARE

Enhancing Clinical Leadership Through Advanced Education

Enhancing clinical leadership through advanced education, particularly via professional doctorates in health and social care, represents a significant development in the landscape of higher education (Open University, 2023). These advanced degrees are designed to meld academic rigour with practical expertise, aiming to equip healthcare professionals not just with enhanced clinical skills, but also with the leadership capabilities necessary to navigate and influence complex healthcare systems (Medical Center of Southeastern Oklahoma, 2024).

Professional doctorates bridge theory and practice, enabling practitioners to apply research directly to clinical settings, thereby improving patient care and outcomes (MacLean, 2024). Furthermore, these programmes foster a culture of continuous learning and innovation among health professionals, encouraging them to question established practices and seek evidence-based improvements (MacLean, 2024). By integrating leadership skills with advanced clinical knowledge, professional doctorates empower healthcare professionals to take on pivotal roles in shaping policies, leading teams effectively, and driving forward the agenda for change within the health and social care sectors (Medical Center of Southeastern Oklahoma, 2024).

This transformative approach ensures that higher education contributes directly to advancing healthcare services, making it more responsive to the needs of patients and society (Medical Center of Southeastern Oklahoma, 2024).

Impact on Healthcare Policy and Systems: A Closer Look

The introduction of professional doctorates in health and social care has been a pivotal development, influencing not just academic circles but also healthcare policies and systems at large (Writer, 2024). These advanced degrees, designed to blend clinical expertise with research, have become instrumental in bridging the gap between theory and practice (Murrays, 2024). Graduates, equipped with both deep practical experience and robust research skills, are uniquely positioned to identify gaps in healthcare delivery and propose evidence-based improvements (New Mexico State University, 2024b).

This dual focus on applied research and practical application has significantly impacted healthcare policy formulation (Indiana University Office of Creative Services, 2024).

As these professionals integrate into the healthcare ecosystem, they bring a fresh perspective that challenges conventional wisdom, advocating for policies that are not only scientifically sound but also practically feasible (Baylor University, 2024). Their work often leads to innovative models of care that prioritise patient outcomes while ensuring efficiency and sustainability within the system (Medical Center of Southeastern Oklahoma, 2024). Consequently, the influence of professional doctorates is reshaping healthcare systems from within, steering them toward more evidence-driven and patient-centred approaches (Fairfield University, 2024).

This evolution marks a crucial shift in how health policies are developed and implemented, promising improvements in service delivery and patient care quality across the board (Anon. 2022).

Challenges and Opportunities in Implementing Professional Doctorates

Implementing professional doctorates in health and social care brings an exclusive set of challenges and opportunities for higher education institutions (University of Hertfordshire, 2023). One of the major hurdles is aligning these programmes with existing academic structures while ensuring they meet professionals' practical, real-world needs (Weckman, 2023). This often involves significantly redesigning curriculum, teaching methods, and assessment strategies to accommodate a blend of rigorous academic research and professional practice that characterises these doctorates (American Association of College of Nursing, 2024).

However, this challenge also presents an opportunity to innovate in educational delivery (Medical College of Georgia, 2024). By fostering closer collaboration between universities and healthcare organisations, professional doctorates can lead to the development of more relevant and impactful research agendas that directly address pressing issues in health and social care (Drexel University, 2024). Furthermore, these programmes offer an avenue for practitioners to advance their skills and knowledge, contributing to workforce development and potentially leading to improved patient outcomes (Medical Center of Southeastern Oklahoma, 2024).

Integrating professional doctorates into higher education thus holds the potential to bridge the gap between theory and practice in the health and social care sectors, despite the considerable implementation challenges involved (Murrays, 2024).

Future Directions for Professional Doctorates in Higher Education

The trajectory of professional doctorates in higher education, especially within health and social care, promises to evolve significantly (University of Derby, 2024). As the demand for advanced practitioners who can navigate complex healthcare environments and address multifaceted social issues grows, institutions may increasingly tailor their programmes toward interdisciplinary learning and research (Fairfield University, 2024). Emphasising practical outcomes alongside theoretical understanding, future professional doctorates could offer more collaborative projects across different sectors, integrating technology and data analytics to solve real-world problems (University of New South Wales, 2024).

Furthermore, there's an anticipated shift towards greater inclusivity and diversity within these programmes, aiming to accurately reflect the communities they serve (Medical Center of Southeastern Oklahoma, 2024). This approach enriches learning experiences and ensures a broader range of perspectives in tackling health and social care challenges (Lazzari, Costley and Nikolou-Walker, 2024). Additionally, as the landscape of higher education changes with digital advancements, we might see more flexible and accessible doctoral programmes that better accommodate working professionals' needs, thereby broadening the scope of who can contribute to advancing their field (Exeed College, 2024).

PROFESSIONAL DOCTORATES BY PUBLIC WORKS

Understanding the Process of Earning a Professional Doctorate Through Publications

Embarking on the journey to earn a professional doctorate through publications is a path less travelled but immensely rewarding for those who pursue it (Open University, 2024). Unlike the traditional doctoral route, which often involves extensive coursework followed by original research culminating in a dissertation, this pathway allows professionals to leverage their existing published work as a foundation for their doctorate (Westminster University, 2024). This approach acknowledges the value of practical, applied research and opens up opportunities for seasoned professionals to contribute to academic knowledge directly from their field of expertise (London School of Economics and Political Science, 2024).

The process of earning a professional doctorate through publications is nuanced and demands a deep understanding of both one's professional domain and the academic requirements set forth by institutions offering such pathways (Coursera, 2024). At its core, this route involves compiling and reflecting upon a portfolio of previously published work that collectively demonstrates significant contributions to the field (Higginbotham, 2024). However, this compilation is not merely an aggregation of one's professional achievements; it requires a critical synthesis that articulates the evolution of thought, application, and impact over time (Higginbotham, 2024).

For many practitioners, this pathway represents an appealing alternative that recognises their sustained commitment to advancing their field through publications such as journal articles, book chapters, policy papers, or other scholarly outputs (Chong and Johnson, 2022). It allows them to achieve academic recognition while continuing their professional commitments (Lee, 2022). The process begins with identifying an academic institution that acknowledges the validity and value of this approach and has provisions for candidates to submit their body of work within specific disciplinary boundaries (Research Topics.com, 2023).

Candidates must then undergo rigorous preparation beyond merely collecting their publications (University of Florida, 2024). They must construct a cohesive narrative that connects each piece of work chronologically and thematically (Mhairi Cowden Associate, 2024). This involves drafting an overarching thesis or argument that binds these individual pieces into a coherent body reflective of doctoral-level scholarship (Research Topics.com, 2023). Such an exercise necessitates critical reflection on one's work in relation to broader disciplinary questions and debates (Glass, 2020).

Furthermore, candidates must demonstrate how their contributions have advanced understanding or practice within their field (Fulton et al., 2019). This often entails engaging deeply with theoretical frameworks and empirical evidence to situate one's work within the wider scholarly community (Open University, 2024). The culmination of this process typically includes presenting this portfolio alongside a substantive piece – often referred to as an exegesis or commentary – which comprehensively explicates the significance and impact of the candidate's work (Tukuniu, 2021).

Earning a professional doctorate through publications thus stands as a testament not only to one's capacity for sustained intellectual contribution but also offers insights into bridging theory with practice effectively (Western Sydney University, 2024). It underscores the importance of applied research in enriching academic discourse while providing seasoned professionals with recognition commensurate with their contributions toward advancing knowledge in tangible ways (Queen Margaret University, 2024).

REFERENCES

Adams, T.E., Homan Jones, S. and Ellis, C. (2022), "Introduction", in Adams, T.E., Homan Jones, S. and Ellis, C. (eds.), *Handbook of Autoethnography*, 2nd ed. London: Routledge.

American Association of College of Nursing (2024), *DPN Education*. Available at: https://www.aacnnursing.org/students/nursing-education-pathways/dnp-education (Accessed: 07 June 2024).

American Psychological Association (2024a), "Definition of Theory", *APA Dictionary of Psychology* (n.d.). Available at: https://dictionary.apa.org/gestalt-psychology (Accessed 07 June 2024).

American Psychological Association (2024b), *APA Dictionary of Psychology: Definition of Gestalt*. American Psychological Association (n.d.). Available at: https://dictionary.apa.org/gestalt (Accessed: 07 March 2024).

Amsalem, D., Duvivier, R. and Martin, A. (2021), "Editorial: Medical education in psychiatry", *Frontiers*. Available at: https://www.frontiersin.org/journals/psychiatry/articles/10.3389/fpsyt.2021.764567/full (Accessed: 07 June 2024).

Anon. (2022), *What is a health policy analyst?, Master's in Public Health Degree Programs*. Available at: https://www.masterspublichealth.net/faq/what-is-a-healthcare-policy-analyst/ (Accessed: 08 June 2024).

Badley, G. (2009), "Publish and be doctor-rated: the PhD by published work", *Quality Assurance in Education*, Vol. 17, No. 4, pp. 331–342.

Bassot, B (2016), *The Reflective Practice Guide*. London: Routledge.

Baylor University (2024), *Why a Baylor PhD?, | Health Services Research | Baylor University*. Available at: https://hankamer.baylor.edu/health-services-phd/why-baylor (Accessed: 08 June 2024).

Ben-Ari, A. and Enosh, G. (2010), "Processes of reflectivity", *Qualitative Social Work*, Vol. 10, No. 2, pp. 152–171.

Berger, R. (2013), "Now I see it, now I don't: Researcher's position and reflexivity in Qualitative Research", *Qualitative Research*, Vol. 15, No. 2, pp. 219–234.

Blaikie, N. and Priest, J. (2017), *Social Research: Paradigms in Action*. Cambridge: Polity Press.

Booth, A. (2006), "Clear and present questions: formulating questions for evidence based practice", *Library Hi Tech*, 2, Vol. 4, No. 3, pp. 355–368.

Bourner, T., Bowden, R.M. and Laing, S. (2001), "Professional doctorates in England", *Studies in Higher Education*, Vol. 26, No. 1, pp. 65–83.

Bradley, E.H. *et al.* (2004), "Translating Research into Clinical Practice: Making Change Happen", *Journal of the American Geriatrics Society*, Vol. 52, No. 11, pp. 1875–1882.

Butt, M. (2013), "One I made earlier: on the PhD by publication", *Text*, Vol. 17 (Special 22). Available at: https://doi.org/10.52086/001c.28309.

Cambridge Dictionary Online (2024), *Gestalt | English Meaning*, Cambridge Dictionary (n.d.). Available at: https://dictionary.

cambridge.org/dictionary/english/gestalt (Accessed: 07 March 2024).

Carayannis, E.G. and Campbell, D.F.J. (2012), "Mode 3 Knowledge Production in Quadruple Helix Innovation Systems", in Carayannis, E.G. and Campbell, D.F.J. (eds.), *Mode 3 Knowledge Production in Quadruple Helix Innovation Systems*. New York, NY: Springer Briefs in Business, Vol. 7.

Cartwright, N. (2020), "Middle-range theory: Without it what could anyone do?", *Theoria*, Vol. 35, No. 3, pp. 269–323.

Chong, S. and Johnson, N. (2022), *Introduction: Demystifying the PhD by publication, University of St Andrews Research Portal*. Available at: https://research-portal.st-andrews.ac.uk/en/publications/introduction-demystifying-the-phd-by-publication (Accessed: 08 June 2024).

Coast, J. and Jackson, L. (2017), "Theoretical and methodological positions and the choice to use qualitative methods", in Coast, J. (ed.), *Qualitative Methods for Health Economics*. London: Rowman & Littlefield.

Collis, J. and Hussey, R. (2014), *Business Research: A Practical Guide for Undergraduate and Postgraduate Students*, 4th ed. London: Palgrave.

Costley, C. (2011), "Professional doctorates and the doctorate of professional studies", in Fell, T., Flint, K. and Haines, I. (eds.), *Professional Doctorates in the U.K.* Lichfield, UK: Council for Graduate Education.

Coursera (2024), *What does 'PhD' stand for?*, *Coursera*. Available at: https://www.coursera.org/articles/what-does-phd-stand-for (Accessed: 08 June 2024).

Dahlberg, K., Dahlberg, H. and Nyström, M. (2013), *Reflective Lifeworld Research*. Studentlitteratur AB.

De Oliveira Lopes, M.V., Da Silva, V.M. and Herdman, T.H. (2015), "Causation and Validation of Nursing Diagnoses: A Middle Range theory", *International Journal of Nursing Knowledge*, Vol. 28, No. 1, pp. 53–59.

Del Giudice, M., Carayannis, E.G. and Della Peruta, M.R. (2011), "Cross-Cultural knowledge management and open innovation diplomacy: The conceptual understanding of knowledge and innovation", in *Innovation, Technology and*

Knowledge Management, Berlin, Springer, pp. 137–152.

Denzin, N.K. (2014), *Interpretive Autoethnography*. London: SAGE.

Dodgson, J.E. (2019), "Reflexivity in qualitative research", *Journal of Human Lactation*, Vol. 35, No. 2, pp. 220–222.

Drexel University (2024), *PhD in Community Health & Prevention, Drexel University Dornsife School of Public Health*. Available at: https://drexel.edu/dornsife/academics/degrees/phd-community-health-and-prevention/ (Accessed: 08 June 2024).

Encyclopaedia Britannica (2024), *Divergent thinking*. Encyclopædia Britannica (n.d.). Available at: https://www.britannica.com/science/divergent-thinking (Accessed: 07 March 2024).

Encyclopedia.Com (2024), *Definition of Middle-Rang Theory*. Available at: https://www.encyclopedia.com/social-sciences/dictionaries-thesauruses-pictures-and-press-releases/middle-range-theory (Accessed: 07 March 2024).

Enders, J. (2005), "Border crossings: Research training, knowledge dissemination and the transformation of academic work", *Higher Education*, Vol. 49, No. 1–2, pp. 119–133.

Exeed College (2024), *Advantages of having a professional doctorate, Exeed College*. Available at: https://exeedcollege.com/blog/advantages-of-having-a-professional-doctorate/ (Accessed: 08 June 2024).

Fairfield University (2024), *Nursing leadership, Fairfield University*. Available at: https://www.fairfield.edu/graduate-and-professional-studies/egan-school-of-nursing-and-health-studies/programs/msn-nursing-leadership/index.html (Accessed: 08 June 2024).

Farrell, T.S. (2013), "Critical incident analysis through narrative reflective practice: A case study", *Iranian Journal of Language Teaching Research*, Vol. 1, No. 1, pp. 79–89.

Fawcett, J. and Garity, J. (2009), *Evaluating Research for Evidence-Based Nursing Practice*. Philadelphia: F.A. Davis.

Francis, D. (1997), "Critical Incident Analysis: a strategy for developing reflective practice", *Teachers and Teaching: Theory and Practice*, Vol. 3, No. 2, pp. 169–188.

Fulton, J., Kuit, J., Sanders, G. and Smith P. (2019), *The Professional Doctorate*. London:

Macmillan International and Red Globe Press.

George Washington University (2024), *MSN: Psychiatric Mental Health Nurse practitioner: School of nursing: The George Washington University, School of Nursing*. Available at: https://nursing.gwu.edu/programs/msn/psychiatric-mental-health-nurse-practitioner (Accessed: 07 June 2024).

Gibbons, M., Limoges, C. and Nowotny, H. (1994), *New Production of Knowledge*. London: SAGE.

Glass, D. (2020) *A doctoral researcher's reflections on Peer Review, Sage Perspectives Blog*. Available at: https://perspectivesblog.sagepub.com/blog/sussex-hive/a-doctoral-researchers-reflections-on-peer-review (Accessed: 09 June 2024).

Green, L., Green, H. and Powell, S. (2005), *Doctoral Study in Contemporary Higher Education*. Maidenhead: McGraw-Hill Education.

Higginbotham, D. (2024), *5 routes to getting a doctorate, Prospects.ac.uk*. Available at: https://www.prospects.ac.uk/postgraduate-study/phd-study/5-routes-to-getting-a-doctorate (Accessed: 08 June 2024).

Indiana University Office of Creative Services, iuweb @ indiana.edu (2024), *IUPUI, Master of Health Administration : IUPUI Bulletins.* Available at: https://bulletins.iu.edu/iupui/2021-2022/schools/public-health/graduate/degrees/mha.shtml (Accessed: 08 June 2024).

Jones, M. (2018), "Contemporary trends in professional doctorates", *Studies in Higher Education*, Vol. 43, No. 5, pp. 814–825.

Kirby, E.A. (2012), "Chapter 2: A conceptual model for Critical Incident Analysis", in Schwester, R.W. (ed.), *Handbook of Critical Incident Analysis*. Oxon: Routledge.

Kolb, D.A. (2015), *Experiential Learning: Experiences as the Source of Learning and Development*. Upper Saddle River: Pearson.

Kuhn, T. (1962), *The Structure of Scientific Revolutions*. Chicago: University of Chicago Press.

Lasuertmer, D. [Internet] (2024), *"40 Best Clinical Practice Doctorates for Social Work - Best MSW Programs"*. Available at: https://www.bestmswprograms.com/top-social-work-doctorate/ (Accessed: 06 June 2024).

Lazzari, C. and Masino, M.A. (2015), *Psicologia e Filosofia della Salute (It.: Health Psychology and Philosophy)*. Milan: libreriauniversitaria.it

Lazzari, C., Nusair, A. and Rabottini, M. (2021). "Chapter 3. Comorbidity and Similarities between Factitious Disorder and Borderline Personality Disorder: Theory, Psychological Assessment, and Management", In: Columbus, A.M. (Ed.), *Advances in Psychology Research, Vol. 146*, New York: Nova.

Lazzari, C., Costley, C. and Nikolou-Walker, E. (2024), *Interprofessional and Intraprofessional Handover and Practice in Healthcare*. Faringdon: Libri.

Lazzari, C. and Shoka, A. (2016a), "Chapter 2. Corporate Management of Patients with Borderline Personality Disorder through Integrated Care", In: Anderson, R. (Ed.), *Borderline Personality Disorder (BPD): Prevalence, Management Options and Challenges*, New York: Nova.

Lazzari, C. and Shoka, A. (2016b), "Chapter 3. Maladaptive Behaviors in Inpatients with Borderline Personality Disorder: A Behavioral Game Theory Explanation",

In: Anderson, R. (Ed.), *Borderline Personality Disorder (BPD): Prevalence, Management Options and Challenges*, New York: Nova.

Lee, S. (2022), *A guide to PhD success: How to thrive during doctoral studies, PhDs. me*. Available at: https://www.phds.me/resources/planning-for-your-phd-doctorate/ (Accessed: 08 June 2024).

Leeman, J. and Sandelowski, M. (2012), "Practice-Based evidence and qualitative inquiry", *Journal of Nursing Scholarship*, Vol. 44, No. 2, pp. 171–179.

Levac, D., Colquhoun, H. and O'Brien, K.K. (2010), "Scoping studies: advancing the methodology", *Implementation Science*, Vol. 5, No. 1, pp. 1–9.

Loma Linda University (2024), *Systems, families, and couples (PhD), School of Behavioral Health*. Available at: https://behavioralhealth.llu.edu/academics/counseling-and-family-sciences/systems-families-and-couples-phd (Accessed: 08 June 2024).

London School of Economics and Political Science (2024), *Application process, Applying for a PhD*. Available at: https://info.lse.ac.uk/

current-students/careers/information-and-resources/application-process/Applying-for-a-phd (Accessed: 08 June 2024).

MacLean, T. (2024), *What is the difference between a professional doctorate and a PhD.?*, Yorkville. Available at: https://www.yorkvilleu.ca/blog/doctorate-vs-phd/ (Accessed: 08 June 2024).

Malthouse, R., Roffey-Barentsen, J. and Watts, M. (2014), "Reflectivity, reflexivity and situated reflective practice", *Professional Development in Education*, Vol. 40, No. 4, pp. 597–609.

Manchester Metropolitan University (2024), *Manchester Metropolitan University: Professional Doctorate in Health and Social Care, Postgrad.* Available at: https://www.postgrad.com/manchester-metropolitan-university-health-professions-professional-doctorate-in-health-and-social-care/course/ (Accessed: 08 June 2024).

Medical Center of Southeastern Oklahoma (2024), *Home, Medical Center of Southeastern Oklahoma*. Available at: https://www.mymcso.com/cultivating-medical-leaders-the-impact-of-advanced-education-programs.html (Accessed: 08 June 2024).

Medical College of Georgia (2024), *Medical College of Georgia*. Available at: https://www.augusta.edu/mcg/ (Accessed: 08 June 2024).

Merriam-Webster Dictionary (2024a), "Deduce definition & meaning", *Merriam-Webster Dictionary Online*, https://www.merriam-webster.com/dictionary/deduce.

Merriam-Webster Dictionary (2024b), "Definition of theory", *Merriam-Webster Dictionary Online*, https://www.merriam-webster.com/dictionary/theory.

Merriam-Webster Dictionary (2024c), "Gestalt definition & meaning", *Merriam-Webster Dictionary Online*, https://www.merriam-webster.com/dictionary/gestalt (Accessed: 07 March 2024).

Mhairi Cowden Associate (2024), *A PhD by publication or how I got my doctorate and kept my sanity, The Conversation*. Available at: https://theconversation.com/a-phd-by-publication-or-how-i-got-my-doctorate-and-kept-my-sanity-11012 (Accessed: 09 June 2024).

Middlesex University (2024), *Masters/Doctor of Professional Studies MProf/DProf*

(Health and Education/Science and Technology)|Middlesex University London, https://www.mdx.ac.uk/courses/postgraduate/doctor-professional-studies.

Mortari L. (2015), "Reflectivity in research practice", *International Journal of Qualitative Methods* 2015; 14: 160940691561804. doi:10.1177/1609406915618045

Mullane, M. (2005), "Demonstrating significance of contribution to professional knowledge and practice in Australian professional doctorate programs: Impacts in the workplace and professions", in Hickey, C., Maxwell, T.W. and Evans, T. (eds.), *Working Doctorates: The Impact of Professional Doctorates in the Workplace and Professions*. Geelong, Victoria, Australia: Research Institute for Professional & Vocational Education & Training.

Murrays, M. (2024), *Bridging theory and practice: Michael Murray's grounded theory approach for doctor of business administration (dbas) and doctor of education (edds)*, LinkedIn. Available at: https://www.linkedin.com/pulse/bridging-theory-practice-michael-murrays-grounded-approach-murray-idpye (Accessed: 08 June 2024).

New Mexico State University (2024a), *Cepy-Counseling & Educational Psychology, New Mexico State University Academic Catalog*. Available at: https://catalogs.nmsu.edu/nmsu/course-listings/cepy/ (Accessed: 07 June 2024).

New Mexico State University (2024b), *Differences between MPH vs MSPH*. Available at: https://global.nmsu.edu/blog/healthcare/difference-between-mph-vs-msph-degree-mph-online-degree/ (Accessed: 06 June 2024)

Nikolou-Walker, E. and Garnett, J. (2004), "Work-based learning. a new imperative: Developing reflective practice in professional life", *Reflective Practice*, Vol. 5, No. 3, pp. 297–312.

Noblit, G.W. and Dwight Hare, R. (1988), *Meta-Ethnography: Synthesizing Qualitative Studies*. Newbury Park, Calif: Sage.

O'Keeffe, P. (2019), "PhD by Publication: innovative approach to social science research, or operationalisation of the doctoral student ... or both?", *Higher*

Education Research and Development, Vol. 39, No. 2, pp. 288–301.

Online Counseling Programs (2024), *How to become a psychologist, CORP-MAC0 (OCP).* Available at: https://onlinecounselingprograms.com/mental-health-careers/how-to-become-psychologist/ (Accessed: 07 June 2024).

Open University (2023), *Doctorate in Health and Social Care (DHSC), Faculty of Wellbeing, Education and Language Studies.* Available at: https://wels.open.ac.uk/research/research-degrees/professional-doctorate-programmes/doctorate-health-and-social-care-dhsc (Accessed: 08 June 2024).

Open University (2024), *Doctoral research: A short introduction, learn1.* Available at: https://learn1.open.ac.uk/mod/oublog/viewpost.php?post=250714 (Accessed: 08 June 2024).

Orlans, V. (2014), "Developing the researching professional", *Higher Education, Skills and Work-based Learning*, Vol. 4, No. 2, pp. 161–170.

Page, M.J. et al. (2021), "The PRISMA 2020 statement: an updated guideline for reporting systematic reviews", *The BMJ*, n71. Available at: https://doi.org/10.1136/bmj.n71.

Park, C., Delgado, C. and Irfan, A. (2023), "Perspectives on the Doctor of Public Health (DrPH) education among students and alumni in the United States: a cross-sectional national online survey", *BMC Public Health* [Internet]. 2023 Aug 16; 23(1). Available at: https://doi.org/10.1186/s12889- 023-16402-3.

Peacock, S. (2017), "The PhD by Publication", *International Journal of Doctoral Studies*, Vol. 12, No. 12, pp. 123–135.

Peters, B. (2021), "Qualitative methods in monitoring and evaluation: The emic and the etic: Their importance to qualitative evaluators", *American University Online*. Available at: https://programs.online.american.edu/msme/masters-in-measurement-and-evaluation/resources/emic-and-etic (Accessed: 07 March 2024).

Peterson, S.J. and Bredow, T.S. (2020), *Middle Range Theories: Application to Nursing*

Research and Practice. Philadelphia: Wolters Kluwer.

Poulos, C.N. (2021), *Autoethnography*. Washington: American Psychological Association.

Powell, S. and Green, H. (Eds) (2007), *The Doctorate Worldwide*, Maidenhead: McGrawHill-Open University Press

Queen Margaret University (2024), *PhD by published work: Retrospective Route Regulations, Queen Margaret University, Edinburgh*. Available at: https://www.qmu.ac.uk/study-here/postgraduate-research-study/graduate-school-and-doctoral-research/phd-by-published-work-retrospective-route-regulations/ (Accessed: 09 June 2024).

Regis College (2023), *What is the psychiatric nurse practitioner job outlook?: Regis College, Regis College Online*. Available at: https://online.regiscollege.edu/online-masters-degrees/online-master-science-nursing/psychiatric-mental-health-nurse-practitioner/resources/psychiatric-nurse-practitioner-job-outlook/ (Accessed: 07 June 2024).

Renjith, V., Yesodharan, R., Noronha J.A., Ladd, E. and George A. (2021), "Qualitative methods in health care research", *International Journal of Preventive Medicine*, Vol. 12, No. 1, pp. 1–7.

Research Topics.com (2023), *PhD by publication – explained, Research Paper Topic Ideas*. Available at: https://www.myresearchtopics.com/guide/phd-by-publication-explained/ (Accessed: 08 June 2024).

Richards, J.C. and Farrell, T.S.C. (2005), *Professional Development for Language Teachers*. New York: Cambridge University Press.

Rolfe, G. and Davies, R. (2009), "Second generation professional doctorate in nursing", *Nurse Education Today*, Vol. 46, No. 9, pp. 1265–1273.

Ross, D.A., Travis, M.J. and Arbuckle, M.R. (2015). "The future of psychiatry as clinical neuroscience: Why not now?", *JAMA Psychiatry*. Available at: https://www.ncbi.nlm.nih.gov/pmc/articles/PMC5347976/ (Accessed: 07 June 2024).

Runco, M.A. and Pritzker, S.R. (eds.) (2011), *Encyclopedia of Creativity*, 2nd ed. London: Elsevier.

Salzman, P.C. (2002), "On reflexivity", *American Anthropologist*, Vol. 104, No. 3, pp. 805–813.

Samuel, P.E. and Stokes, D. (2023), "Creativity", in Zalta, E.N. and Nodelman, U. (eds.), *The Stanford Encyclopedia of Philosophy* [online], https://plato.stanford.edu/archives/spr2023/entries/creativity/.

Schwester, R.W., Horning, A.M. and Dank, M. (2012), "Chapter 3: Conceptualising and defining critical incidents", in Schwester, R.W. (ed.), *Handbook of Critical Incident Analysis*. Oxon: Routledge.

Smith, M.J., Liehr, P.R. and Carpenter, R.D. (2024), *Middle Range Theory for Nursing*. New York: Springer Publishing Company.

Smith, S. (2015), *PhD by Published Work*. London: Palgrave.

Thompson, S. and Thompson, N. (2018), *The Critically Reflective Practitioners*, 2nd ed. London: Palgrave.

Tukuniu, D. (2021), *PhD by Prior Publication – Information for prospective applicants, Research*. Charles Sturt University. Available at: https://research.csu.edu.au/

resources/guides/students/phd-by-prior-publication-information-for-prospective-applicants (Accessed: 09 June 2024).

University of Dayton (2024), *Counselor Education and Human Services <UDayton*. Available at: https://catalog.udayton.edu/graduate/schoolofeducationandhealthsciences/programsofstudy/counseloreducationandhumanservices/.

University of Derby (2024), *Dr Alan R Williams programme leader, Health, Social and Community Work - University of Derby*. Available at: https://www.derby.ac.uk/online/health-social-community-work-courses/doctor-health-social-care-practice/ (Accessed: 08 June 2024).

University of Florida (2024), *Graduate Catalog, Graduate Degrees & lt; University of Florida*. Available at: https://gradcatalog.ufl.edu/graduate/degrees/ (Accessed: 08 June 2024).

University of Hertfordshire (2023), *Doctorate in Health and Social Care, Research|Uni of Herts*. Available at: https://www.herts.ac.uk/courses/research/doctorate-in-health-and-social-care (Accessed: 08 June 2024).

University of Miami (2024), *Psychology (psy), University of Miami Academic Bulletin*. Available at: https://bulletin.miami.edu/courses-az/psy/ (Accessed: 07 June 2024).

University of Nevada (2022), *Role of social workers in Mental Health, University of Nevada, Reno*. Available at: https://onlinedegrees.unr.edu/blog/role-of-social-workers-in-mental-health/ (Accessed: 07 June 2024).

University of New South Wales (2024), *Professional Doctorate: UNSW Sydney, UNSW Sites*. Available at: https://www.unsw.edu.au/research/hdr/professional-doctorate (Accessed: 08 June 2024).

University of Ohio (2024), *From RN to BSN: A path to nursing leadership and career advancement, OHIO News*. Available at: https://www.ohio.edu/news/2024/05/rn-bsn-path-nursing-leadership-and-career-advancement (Accessed: 07 June 2024).

University of Southern California (USC) (2024), *Doctor of education in mental health leadership (online), USC Rossier School of Education*. Available at: https://rossier.usc.edu/programs/find-compare-programs/

doctor-education-mental-health-leadership-online (Accessed: 07 June 2024).

Weckman, A. (2023), Doctorate or PhD? *what's the difference?: Ubis Global, UBIS University of Business Innovation and Sustainability.* Available at: https://ubisglobal.com/blog/doctorate-or-phd-whats-the-difference/ (Accessed: 08 June 2024).

Weingart, P. (1998), "Science and the media", *Research Policy*, Vol. 27, No. 8, pp. 869–879.

Western Sydney University (2024), *Doctor of philosophy by publication rule, Doctor of Philosophy by Publication Rule / Document / Policy DDS.* Available at: https://policies.westernsydney.edu.au/document/view.current.php?id=165&version=1 (Accessed: 09 June 2024).

Westminster University (2024), PhD by published work, PhD by published work | University of Westminster, London. Available at: https://www.westminster.ac.uk/study/postgraduate/research-degrees/mode-of-study/phd-by-published-work (Accessed: 08 June 2024).

Writer, S. (2024), *25 best health policy programs*

PhD, The Best Health Degrees. Available at: https://www.besthealthdegrees.com/best-health-care-management-phd/ (Accessed: 08 June 2024).

Writers, S. (2024), *Clinical Psychology Ph.D. Program Guide* [Internet]. Psychology.org | Psychology's Comprehensive Online Resource. 2024. Available at: https://www.psychology.org/degrees/clinical-psychology/phd/ (Accessed: 06 June 2024).

www.ingramcontent.com/pod-product-compliance
Lightning Source LLC
Chambersburg PA
CBHW032132090426
42743CB00007B/576